I0820528

I Picked These for You

Written by: M.H. Clark
Illustrated by: Cécile Metzger

I was thinking today just how much of the time
there are thoughts of you floating around in my mind.

And I wanted to show you how grateful I am
that you're here, that you're you, that you're such a dear friend.

Hmm, I pondered, there's got to be some little way
to express how completely you brighten each day.

Something more than a card... longer lasting than cake...
something brilliant and big as the difference you make.

Something made all for you, not just pulled from a shelf.
Maybe flowers? I thought, I could pick them myself...

I could choose all the ones that remind me of you.
And I knew, right away, that was just what I'd do.

To start with, some roses, 'cause roses felt right—
just like you, they are always a perfect delight.

Then forget-me-nots, for all the good memories
of the wonderful moments that you've shared with me.

Then some lilies—they seemed like the loveliest friends,
which is perfect because that is *just* who you've been.

Oh, some daisies! I thought, these might offer a smile.
(Because that is what you've offered me, this whole while.)

I found irises, perfectly one of a kind,
each so rare and unique that they brought you to mind.

Then some sunflowers—so vibrant, strong, and sincere
that it felt for a moment like you were right here.

So I tucked them all in and I hurried along...
There was still such a great deal of work to be done!

I picked big flowers, small flowers, known and unknown.
And all of a sudden, my armful had grown.

But the truth is a small bouquet isn't enough
for someone who matters so deeply, so much.

And each time I remembered who all this was for,
I kept wanting to add in a little bit more.

So... that's how I ended up with all of these.
Each one is for you, full of love, straight from me.

Because flowers spread joy everywhere they exist.
And you know what? You're also quite gifted at this.

Just like flowers, you brighten each place that you go...
And you do this more fully than I think you know.

So, I picked these for you, and I hope in some way
they might perk up and sweeten and gladden your day.

Because that is exactly what you do for me,
all the time, every day. It's just part of your being.

An imprint of the Crown Publishing Group
A division of Penguin Random House LLC
1745 Broadway, New York, NY 10019
live-inspired.com | penguinrandomhouse.com

ISBN: 978-1-957891-63-7

Writer: M.H. Clark
Illustrator: Cécile Metzger
Editor: Bailey Vega
Art Director: Megan Gandt
Production Manager: Olivia Holmes

1st printing. Manufactured in China with soy inks on FSC®-Mix certified paper.

The authorized representative in the EU for product safety and compliance is Penguin Random House Ireland, Morrison Chambers, 32 Nassau Street, Dublin D02 YH68, Ireland, https://eu-contact.penguin.ie.

Create meaningful moments with gifts that inspire.

CONNECT WITH US
live-inspired.com | sayhello@compendiuminc.com

@compendiumliveinspired
#compendiumliveinspired